W9-BCX-907

DATE DUE

Let's Read About Our Bodies
Conozcamos nuestro cuerpo

Nose/Nariz

Cynthia Klingel & Robert B. Noyed
photographs by/fotografías por Gregg Andersen

Reading consultant/Consultora de lectura: Cecilia Minden-Cupp, Ph.D.,
Adjunct Professor, College of Continuing and Professional Studies, University of Virginia

For a free color catalog describing Weekly Reader® Early Learning Library's list of high-quality books, call 1-877-445-5824 or fax your request to (414) 336-0164.

Library of Congress Cataloging-in-Publication Data

Klingel, Cynthia.
   Nose = Nariz / by Cynthia Klingel and Robert B. Noyed. — [Bilingual ed.]
      p. cm. — (Let's read about our bodies = Conozcamos nuestro cuerpo)
   Includes bibliographical references and index.
   Summary: A bilingual introduction to the nose, what it is used for, and how to take care of it.
   ISBN 0-8368-3077-6 (lib. bdg.)
   ISBN 0-8368-3326-0 (softcover)
   1. Nose—Juvenile literature. [1. Nose. 2. Smell. 3. Senses and sensation. 4. Spanish language materials—Bilingual.] I. Title: Nariz. II. Noyed, Robert B. III. Title.
   QM505.K565   2002
   611'.21—dc21   2001055095

This edition first published in 2002 by
Weekly Reader® Early Learning Library
330 West Olive Street, Suite 100
Milwaukee, WI 53212 USA

An Editorial Directions book
Editors: E. Russell Primm and Emily Dolbear
Translators: Tatiana Acosta and Guillermo Gutiérrez
Art direction, design, and page production: The Design Lab
Photographer: Gregg Andersen
Weekly Reader® Early Learning Library art direction: Tammy Gruenewald
Weekly Reader® Early Learning Library page layout: Katherine A. Goedheer

Printed in the United States of America

2 3 4 5 6 7 8 9 06 05 04 03 02

Note to Educators and Parents

As a Reading Specialist I know that books for young children should engage their interest, impart useful information, and motivate them to want to learn more.

Let's Read About Our Bodies is a new series of books designed to help children understand the value of good health and of taking care of their bodies.

A young child's active mind is engaged by the carefully chosen subjects. The imaginative text works to build young vocabularies. The short, repetitive sentences help children stay focused as they develop their own relationship with reading. The bright, colorful photographs of children enjoying good health habits complement the text with their simplicity to both entertain and encourage young children to want to learn — and read — more.

These books are designed to be used by adults as "read-to" books to share with children to encourage early literacy in the home, school, and library. They are also suitable for more advanced young readers to enjoy on their own.

Una nota a los educadores y a los padres

Como especialista en lectura, sé que los libros infantiles deben interesar a los niños, proporcionar información útil y motivarlos a aprender.

Conozcamos nuestro cuerpo es una nueva serie de libros pensada para ayudar a los niños a entender la importancia de la salud y del cuidado del cuerpo.

Los temas, cuidadosamente seleccionados, mantienen ocupada la activa mente del niño. El texto, lleno de imaginación, facilita el enriquecimiento del vocabulario infantil. Las oraciones, breves y repetitivas, ayudan a los niños a centrarse en la actividad mientras desarrollan su propia relación con la lectura. Las bellas fotografías de niños que disfrutan de buenos hábitos de salud complementan el texto con su sencillez, y consiguen entretener a los niños y animarlos a aprender nuevos conceptos y a leer más.

Estos libros están pensados para que los adultos se los lean a los niños, con el fin de fomentar la lectura incipiente en el hogar, en la escuela y en la biblioteca. También son adecuados para que los jóvenes lectores más avanzados los disfruten leyéndolos por su cuenta.

Cecilia Minden-Cupp, Ph.D., Adjunct Professor,
College of Continuing and Professional Studies, University of Virginia

This is my nose. I like to wiggle my nose.

- - - - - - -

Ésta es mi nariz. Me gusta mover la nariz.

I use my nose to smell
lots of things.

— — — — — — —

Uso la nariz para oler
muchas cosas.

Some things smell yummy.

Algunas cosas huelen deliciosas.

Some things smell stinky!

¡Algunas cosas huelen asquerosas!

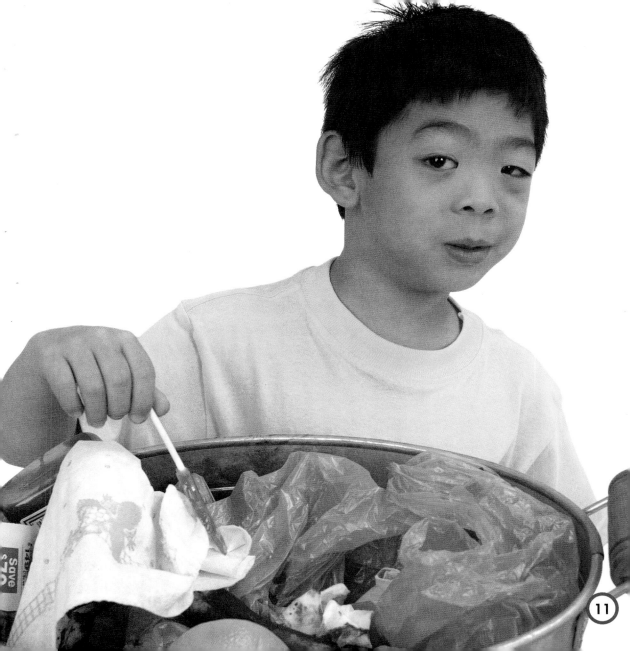

I use my nose to breathe.

Uso la nariz para respirar.

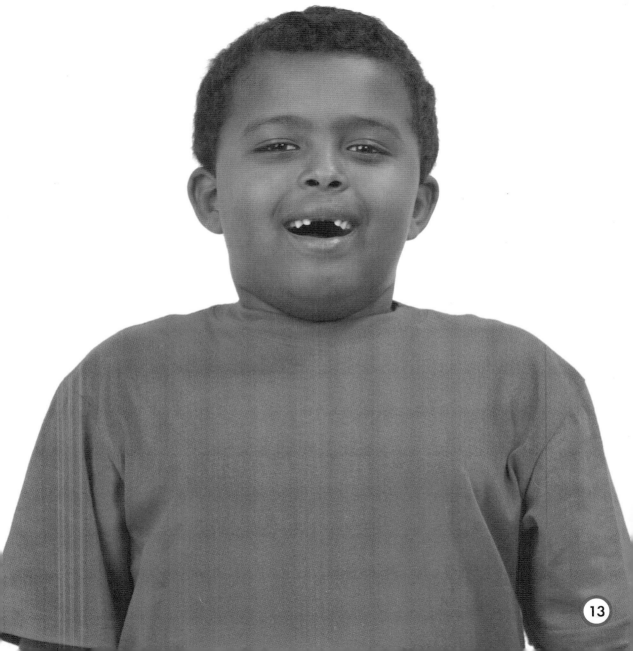

Some things make me sneeze. Pepper, flour, and dust make me sneeze.

_____

Algunas cosas me hacen estornudar. La pimienta, la harina y el polvo me hacen estornudar.

Sometimes I get a stuffy nose.

A veces se me tapa la nariz.

Sometimes I have a runny nose. Then I need to wipe my nose.

— — — — — — — —

A veces me moquea la nariz. Entonces, tengo que sonarme la nariz.

I am careful to take care of my nose.

Tengo mucho cuidado de mi nariz.

Glossary/Glosario

breathe—to take air into the lungs and then let it out
respirar—tomar aire en los pulmones y soltarlo

sneeze—air forced from the nose and mouth in a sudden way
estornudo—aire que echamos por la nariz y la boca de manera inesperada

stuffy—closed up
tapada—cerrada

yummy—good tasting
deliciosa—que sabe bien

For More Information/Más información

Fiction Books/Libros de ficción
Brown, Marc Tolon. *Arthur's Nose*. Boston:
   Little Brown & Co., 1986.
Caple, Kathy. *The Biggest Nose*. Boston:
   Houghton Mifflin Co., 1988.
Faulkner, Keith. *The Long-Nosed Pig*. New York:
   Dial Books for Young Readers, 1998.

Nonfiction Books/Libros de no ficción
Fowler, Allan. *Knowing about Noses*. New York:
   HarperCollins Juvenile Books, 1991.
Moses, Brian. *Munching, Crunching, Sniffling,
   and Snooping*. New York: DK Publishing, 1999.

Web Sites/Páginas Web
What's That Smell? The Nose Knows
kidshealth.org/kid/body/nose_SW.html
For information about the different parts of the nose

Index/Índice

About the Authors/Información sobre los autores

Cynthia Klingel has worked as a high school English teacher and an elementary school teacher. She is currently the curriculum director for a Minnesota school district. Cynthia Klingel lives with her family in Mankato, Minnesota.

Cynthia Klingel ha trabajado como maestra de inglés de secundaria y como maestra de primaria. Actualmente es la directora de planes de estudio de un distrito escolar de Minnesota. Cynthia Klingel vive con su familia en Mankato, Minnesota.

Robert B. Noyed started his career as a newspaper reporter. Since then, he has worked in school communications and public relations at the state and national level. Robert B. Noyed lives with his family in Brooklyn Center, Minnesota.

Robert B. Noyed comenzó su carrera como reportero en un periódico. Desde entonces ha trabajado en comunicación escolar y relaciones públicas a nivel estatal y nacional. Robert B. Noyed vive con su familia en Brooklyn Center, Minnesota.